WORDS OF THE CHAMPIONS
YOUR KEY TO THE BEE

2020

Contents

Developed by the Scripps National Spelling Bee
Copyright 2019, Scripps National Spelling Bee

Greetings, Champions!

About this Study Guide

Do you dream of winning a school spelling bee, or even attending the Scripps National Spelling Bee? *Words of the Champions* is the official study resource of the Scripps National Spelling Bee, so you've found the perfect place to start. Prepare for a 2019 or 2020 classroom, grade-level, school, district, county, regional or state spelling bee with this list of 4,000 words.

All words in this book have been selected by the Scripps National Spelling Bee from our official dictionary, *Merriam-Webster Unabridged* (http://unabridged.merriam-webster.com).

Words of the Champions is divided into three difficulty levels, ranked One Bee (800 words), Two Bee (2,100 words) and Three Bee (1,200 words). These are great words to challenge you, whether you're just getting started in spelling bees or of if you've already participated in several. At the beginning of each level, you'll find the *School Spelling Bee Study List* words. For any classroom, grade-level or school spelling bee, study the 125-word One Bee *School Spelling Bee Study List*, the 225-word Two Bee *School Spelling Bee Study List* and the 100-word Three Bee *School Spelling Bee Study List:* a total of 450 words.

Following the *School Spelling Bee Study List* in each level, you'll find pages marked "Words of the Champions." Are you a school spelling bee champion or a speller advancing to compete beyond the school level? Study these pages to make sure you're prepared to do your best when these words are asked in the early rounds of competition. And remember, although spelling bees will start with words from this guide, they often end with words you haven't studied.

Each year, the Scripps National Spelling Bee will release a new version of *Words of the Champions* featuring 800 new words, including an all-new *School Spelling Bee Study List*.

Your spelling bee journey starts now, and taking the first step toward becoming a star athlete of the English language makes you a *Champion*. These *Words* are for you.

About the Scripps National Spelling Bee

The Scripps National Spelling Bee is the nation's largest and longest-running educational program. The purpose of the Scripps National Spelling Bee is to help students improve their spelling, increase their vocabularies, learn concepts and develop correct English usage that will help them all their lives.

Visit spellingbee.com for more information about the Bee and to check if your school is enrolled. The Scripps National Spelling Bee is administered on a not-for-profit basis by The E.W. Scripps Company.

Difficulty Level: One Bee
School Spelling Bee Study List

punting	jolly	giant
crowd	powder	sniffle
secret	walnut	mouth
fumble	sawdust	filters
pond	flustered	cone
health	barber	never
pardon	chimes	silly
shake	cabin	Monday
kiddo	faint	grub
proof	manger	hook
gorp	peppermint	number
town	broth	cooking
bingo	ash	amazed
clever	flame	collect
inside	grits	local
reply	cliff	proper
frozen	hem	basement
special	candles	ripple
film	brim	feats
results	plot	plumbing
soda	desk	stubborn
seal	bobcat	adrift
twirled	polo	sweeten
admit	roller	neon
grown-ups	stark	beeswax
pieces	drum	social
brass	snarl	behold
onshore	argue	mix
stunts	loppers	drool
deny	petal	understand

sound	jangled	finish
benches	chain	cheer
shrugged	workhorse	twisty
still	antennas	chips
pranks	honest	scoop
smiled	holler	rover
peach	billboard	forgive
pie	chicken	ribbon
size	puppets	shoo
hall	waited	greedy
		beam
		crew
		crate
		hotel
		stray

Great Words, Great Works Reading Program

Each year, the Scripps National Spelling Bee publishes its School Spelling Bee Study List to help students prepare for classroom and school-level spelling bees. These words come from a list of books carefully selected by the Bee's editorial team. That list of books is called Great Words, Great Works. Find it at spellingbee.com/book-list.

Difficulty Level: One Bee
Words of the Champions

gradual	turtle	bogus
ferocious	Pinkerton	recoup
frequently	fortune	bookworm
permission	sluggard	veteran
towel	bedlam	erase
sundae	shortfall	handcuffs
ornament	cowlick	spinal
rooster	opinionated	demolition
scold	slogan	gargantuan
organza	triumphant	salsa
fragile	parenthetic	chaotic
galaxy	listener	shrimp
complaint	guardian	mandate
curries	dwindled	turret
tennis	fraught	pigeon
grumbling	sturdy	satellite
garlic	treadmill	parasite
hula	originate	favorite
reactionary	forfend	OR *favourite
muscular	OR forefend	cascade
drizzle	eavesdrop	dandelion
accurate	January	famous
studio	scruple	pristine
illusionist	moxie	golden
genetic	winnow	modesty
levity	incentive	amphibian
moisture	admirer	jealousy
toughness	emotional	remedial
tasteless	chia	vouch
astute	raspberry	trivia

*chiefly British spelling

shoulder	freight	genius
zebra	honeybee	nuance
butterscotch	blemish	stencil
apron	crumpet	penguin
beagle	blizzard	freckle
kidney	squirm	blooper
wistful	harmonious	misconception
raven	lawyer	lambkin
fructose	valiant	chowder
Amazon	purse	sunflower
companion	raisin	lambasted
panorama	trumpet	volumetric
gimmick	bias	flattery
flannel	lettuce	simmer
cucumber	shamrock	whisk
McMansion	Americana	bathtub
janitor	monopolize	fantastically
lionize	water	failure
headdress	marathon	tolerable
fragrance	omission	mosquito
pear	newbie	target
system	spreadsheet	angora
pedigree	badger	snippet
empty	fortification	ascribe
amulet	hydra	hodgepodge
guess	grouse	verbiage
magician	manta	nephew
carrot	astonish	imbibe
meteor	fashionista	savvy
distraught	stubble	reckon

In Good Company

When it comes to spelling bee participants, the more the merrier! In fact, more than 11 million spellers participate in qualifying spelling bees throughout the country and around the world.

---

boorish	tantrum	graham
tarmac	science	headlong
iteration	cement	timber
nurture	venomous	medallion
volcano	plaintiff	maximum
forensics	mayhem	clover
miraculous	thicket	casino
trendy	gymnastics	distinctive
permafrost	island	mister
iceberg	peacenik	warning
cactus	ounce	useful
nationalism	memorandum	difficult
leeway	bother	mischief
pilferer	missile	talent
rollicking	munchkin	kiwi
quart	banana	publish
lactose	furnace	mutter
domineering	foothills	sedentary
onion	tongue	divine
abandon	caterpillar	lexicon
jamboree	wasp	bristle
junior	kudos	daresay
hamlet	alpha	owlishly
jubilant	shebang	criminal
thawed	tibia	recipient
uncle	hazelnut	strong
dawdle	votive	canteen
mogul	lantern	aviation
troll	mince	lucky
kindred	bubbly	rocket

reflect	measly	glimpse
scent	apprehensive	magnate
puzzles	zither	hangnail
scumble	whiff	novelist
extinct	organic	sourly
jersey	mugwump	serpentine
trapezoid	dollars	taco
dillydally	hospitality	melodramatic
haggle	necklace	sirloin
sword	explanation	deodorant
mastiff	thimblerig	dojo
cooperate	landmark	conductor
merchandise	peerless	garment
gauntlet	flute	ladybug
apology	skateboard	bebop
carnival	manifesto	nuisance
buffoonery	imitative	saga
intellectual	famished	lookout
tickled	ecotourism	blouse
domino	cancel	relish
ignite	flooey	propaganda
legacy	ginger	foxes
splurge	lifetime	ragamuffin
neigh	integrity	ingredient
cabbage	arcade	generosity
erode	manufacture	religious
formalize	bellyache	timidly
OR *formalise	keyhole	bargain
anyway	seldom	around
isolation	impostor	wan
	OR imposter	

*chiefly British spelling

Our Namesake

Although the first national spelling bee occurred in 1925, it wasn't until 1941 that Scripps-Howard Newspapers, now known as The E.W. Scripps Company, assumed leadership of the program.

faculty	winsome	problem
spelunker	trencher	acorn
major	compilation	cutlery
methodology	dandruff	ambitious
weevil	widget	monumental
innermost	goblet	basilisk
aromatherapy	gander	lamentable
peekaboo	slipshod	brilliant
beckon	pencil	competitive
rhinestone	granola	lounge
mundane	monarch	supper
magnificent	jargon	explosive
flexible	incendiary	cajole
skeleton	Velcro	bauble
weakness	award	happenstance
priority	parsley	tussle
third	rascal	inched
ovation	ravine	dimension
sonar	perplex	ugliness
beverage	qualitative	quack
stench	sticky	spider
yarn	hamstring	weather
hubbub	vacuum	twinge
premium	reliable	poncho
sinus	snore	hooligan
trait	ladle	decade
swallow	surefire	forbidden
recyclable	enchantment	jumbo
turnip	apple	mortal
tirade	mellow	bugaboo
materialize	nacho	standard

yearn	balderdash	dauntlessly
primatologist	infringe	faucet
voluntary	interloper	scheme
furious	routine	cough
wombat	privacy	straw
marginalize	decision	hooves
swipe	farfetched	shadow
eternity	linen	meekness
imagery	piratical	squall
pastel	pigsty	OR squawl
twice	misery	omen
megahertz	months	militant
gnash	guffaw	civics
knuckle	caravan	locker
bribery	culinary	jabberwocky
glucose	boycott	detention
mower	calzone	sparkle
campus	bawl	calico
infant	circle	theme
thunderbolt	respect	literacy
despicable	introverted	loathe
elderly	fuddy-duddy	axle
amigo	pulley	glimmer
bestow	Kodiak	vacation
gung ho	misinterpret	napkin
umbrella	twee	overrun
synthetic	holiday	yellowfin
cloying	indigo	clodhopper
olive	forage	crayon
truth	tooth	bakery

Cruising the Airwaves

The first broadcast of the Bee wasn't on television — it was on radio! It wasn't until 1946 that it was first televised. ESPN started airing the Scripps National Spelling Bee in 1994.

porridge	bombard	Romeo
eyelet	furtive	emerge
yeti	journal	twitchy
groove	tulip	arrogant
estimate	myself	normative
cattail	marine	homework
paraphrase	cloudy	mildew
heartthrob	cricket	pattern
cheek	motto	coffee
daughter	torch	botch
laser	pamper	receptacle
invoke	pleasant	bagpipe
upshot	robin	bonfire
climate	historical	abruptly
yankee	rules	bushel
dim sum	geometric	skedaddle
moose	villa	toddler
cuckoo	midriff	everglades
dilemma	teaspoon	pellet
outrageous	worrywart	klutz
silver	developer	envoy
fedora	shopaholic	postpone
wildcat	magma	wafer
monstrosity	briefcase	software
sofa	deputy	factoid
eggplant	mangrove	marvelous
kosher	enfranchise	OR marvellous
minority	kiln	evince
default	webisode	season
heroic	kangaroo	horizon

arborio
cartoon
dough
emperor
utterable
leniency
frivolous
potato
wholehearted
metadata

knock
whittle
joyful
genuine
recluse
shield
tiger
romaine
migraine
oasis

farewell
hypnotic
jewel
tangible
nourish
vulpine
aloha
entrance
kindergarten
restaurant

navigator
humane
polenta
delicacy
noggin
background
thistle

functionary
dodge
iota
gelato
hankering
esteem
knack
satisfactory
barefoot
trope

The 93rd Scripps National Spelling Bee

Mark your calendar! The Scripps National Spelling Bee will take place from May 24-29, 2020, at the Gaylord National Resort & Convention Center in Oxon Hill, Maryland, near Washington, D.C.

Difficulty Level: Two Bee
School Spelling Bee Study List

gallop

dinosaur

brought

ancient

earthquake

tapestry

delivery

attagirl

salamanders

disembark

usual

challenge

cahoots

oozing

Mars

pelican

drastic

yoga

burlap

blazer

trombone

trembling

calmed

police

certain

barograph

charred

Pakistan

pressure

surmised

teak

transit

cannonade

appetite

luggage

ramparts

vinyl

anemometers

dainty

buckle

vividly

briny

pavement

garnet

furrow

sprawl

museum

wren

legend

transistor

amplify

security

refrain

tactics

shepherd

Angus

mulish

rivalry

siblings

chestnut

minivan

plaid

tissue

scoundrel

amino

menthol

Tabasco

obvious

pulse

cottage

garland

gnaw

comfort

caroling

OR carolling

foolishness

constellation

sundering

juncture

exploits

rabble-rouser

profound

wreath

profile

untoward

memorial

industrial

barrier

gratingly

brayed

Harlem	fearsome	diminished
messenger	fiercest	organist
beacons	residence	operator
generation	abated	Louisiana
coverage	scattering	perpetual
deters	toppled	blustery
Nepal	vane	molars
disinfectant	vortices	arrange
campaign	turbulent	dissolved
starvation	obstacles	extremely
gamma	continental	plastic
spleen	deportment	multiplication
utensils	exhibits	middle
depot	agricultural	reasonable
incident	momentous	closet
brambles	disturbance	investigation
trifecta	wily	accident
shingle	rookie	discussion
mason	transparencies	confused
avoid	hazmat	microwave
static	Antarctic	gabled
samples	perfume	settle
modern	plaiting	somber
chalk	writers	OR sombre
concentrate	series	tampered
proud	audience	loyal
expiration	insubstantial	remarkable
batteries	staggered	joists
centuries	assistance	scrambling
differed	sanitized	inspector

distressed
smudge
throttle
perfection
capable
gadgets
channel
chisel
chimney
minnow

domain
shuffle
carpenter
pruners
parcel
squawk
Sheetrock
trowel
nervous
spirit

equator
evidence
solar
explore
distance
fault
colonists
prudence
assembly
sheriff

tarry
entity
archives
commotion
vacancy
beatboxing
mutate
commonplace
gingerbread
hunky-dory

dispute
episode
confection
autographs
withers
petite
station

A Big Time Spellebrity
If you've watched the Bee on ESPN, you've probably seen his face. You've definitely heard his voice. We're talking about the official pronouncer of the Bee, Dr. Jacques Bailly. He won the Scripps National Spelling Bee in 1980 and took up the role of pronouncer in 2003.

Difficulty Level: Two Bee
Words of the Champions

hexagonal	choreographer	inundate
litmus	leguminous	wunderkind
seethe	ceramics	filial
antiquarian	mimetic	wearisome
phalanges	unabated	visage
bachelorette	petrifying	fascinator
frontier	specimen	testimony
unctuous	interlocutor	beaucoup
fluoride	machete	banal
moorage	dulcet	seismologist
Minotaur	salubrious	spectacles
intermezzo	rotisserie	innovator
edification	**paneer	bursary
vacuousness	OR panir	hallowed
epilepsy	omnibus	apogee
importunate	biscotti	hiatus
recuperation	calibrate	freesia
citronella	appellation	exoneration
palliative	duodenum	duvet
abhorrence	valorous	turpitude
personnel	isotopic	platitude
vexatious	carpal	nobiliary
faux	quizzical	commerce
sophisticated	heliotrope	keratitis
nebulous	squander	honorific
genus	prenuptial	kookaburra
legionnaire	succulent	napoleon
sternutation	bedraggled	superlative
subcutaneous	rectitude	oxygenate
alacrity	uranium	annihilate

**preferred spelling

sarcophagus
surrogate
terabyte
uncouth
onerous
macrocosm
bulbous
umpirage
heredity
philharmonic

**bandanna
OR bandana
manipulable
axiomatic
indefatigable
ulterior
oligarchy
pianola
dignify
allegiance

whimsical
stamina
criteria
reprieve
consequent
contusion
mulligan
sabermetrics
elocution
dowager

endorphin
pharmacy
fondant
cupola
herbaceous
tentativeness
pachinko
decrepitude
redux
dramaturgy

basaltic
scorpion
planetarium
ecstatic
cinnamon
pharaoh
opponency
referendum
quaver
rabbinic

comparison
diaphanous
agoraphobia
buffet
tortoise
surmountable
endure
bonobo
abrogate
effusive

murmuration
Clydesdale
phonics
calisthenics
obediential
odiferous
combination
torrent
arsenic
invertebrate

lapel
mackerel
callow
biscuit
flourish
beatific
repository
dissipate
accomplice
kerchief

primitive
fabulist
comportment
taciturn
sophomoric
laureate
Goliath
splenetic
legato
slovenly

Our Purpose

The purpose of the Bee is to help students improve their spelling, increase their vocabularies, learn concepts and develop correct English usage that will help them all their lives.

aerobics	ghastly	achromatic
paisley	parkour	miscible
contrariwise	fealty	soprano
petroleum	perilous	cutis
regalia	steroid	hyrax
incinerate	gullibility	truncheon
flagon	tarantula	educand
incoherent	cantankerous	Realtor
tercentenary	vitriolic	billabong
vituperative	crinoline	bariatrics
churlish	debris	throughout
riviera	armaments	propulsion
laconic	versatile	assailant
excision	subtlety	charioteer
emblazoned	hangar	solicit
bric-a-brac	verbena	melismatic
longitude	zirconium	spurious
maverick	ventriloquy	tempeh
retrograde	circumflex	statistician
partridge	calligram	ibuprofen
insignia	eczema	injurious
binomial	theomachy	anglophile
luminance	fibula	defiant
adjective	aberration	substitute
elucidate	necrotic	quiddity
spatula	eminent	karst
triglycerides	demographics	Brigadoon
stalwart	Jurassic	vestibule
bumptious	myoglobin	ballyhooed
farcical	frugal	arpeggio

lupine	alpaca	filbert
resuscitate	duress	Galahad
approbatory	eucalyptus	jadeite
catalepsy	rambunctious	peripheral
labyrinthine	ingenuous	elevator
notoriety	phonetician	chaperonage
subterranean	macular	frittata
aubergine	simpatico	vandalize
jalapeño	adhesion	chancellor
attributive	rennet	pauper
plutonomy	pinnacle	epoch
lobotomy	avalanche	dumbwaiter
assumption	cadge	allergenic
entrepreneur	exodus	vocabulary
besieged	philosophize	vassal
placoderm	Requiem	panary
hermitage	glitterati	tangerine
permutation	transference	pervasive
conference	uveal	haphazard
woebegone	candelabrum	legislature
resplendence	vacillate	shenanigans
aphasia	phenotype	inclusion
environs	transposable	physicists
celebratory	thrasonical	tempura
cornucopia	trepanation	reggae
prominent	Holstein	futility
archetype	quadrillion	untenable
travails	tardigrade	feudalism
antipathy	varsity	malevolent
leviathan	scholarship	posada

Sharing the Spotlight
The Scripps National Spelling Bee has declared co-champions in 1950, 1957, 1962, 2014, 2015, 2016 and 2019. Diana Reynard and Colquitt Dean were the first co-champs in 1950.

acquiesce	astrobleme	oblique
apothecary	sabotage	buoyancy
summary	absolution	situation
brogue	rutabaga	lumbar
suet	espousal	topiary
koto	virulence	reverberant
jingoism	allocable	yeanling
satchel	effraction	homicide
evanescent	limousine	graphologist
diverge	drupiferous	principality
exemplar	organelle	Nostradamus
marsupial	osprey	taxonomic
trefoil	elusive	beret
designer	disproportionate	talisman
leisure	cayenne	impecunious
vague	tabernacle	reciprocity
wharf	phosphorescent	molecule
altercation	anxiety	millennial
fratority	conch	ineffable
cataclysmic	singultus	abnegation
metatarsal	impromptu	beguile
bereavement	oracle	centenary
carbohydrates	condemn	matrimony
sesame	scenographer	errata
palatable	neuroticism	stipulate
gratis	cannoli	naïveté
nonvolatile	platoon	OR naiveté
juvenilia	solstice	cadence
fomentation	swannery	fido
reprisal	probative	vehicular

sabbatical	muchacha	affront
ermine	steppe	element
pugilist	palpitant	desolate
tapioca	nonchalance	truncate
festooned	realm	pedicure
tectonic	estuary	**caftan
wizened	technician	OR kaftan
tomfoolery	dietetic	ingratiate
harrumph	homage	sousaphone
embezzlement	cumulus	amalgam
fallacy	essential	carnage
asylum	seraphic	turmeric
remuneration	cameist	zoolatry
expostulate	scrumptiously	ricochet
integument	toploftical	hackneyed
Hebrides	noctambulist	vespertine
macaw	visibility	**brusque
perspicacious	ligament	OR brusk
reimbursable	plenitude	erstwhile
jambalaya	illustrious	lolled
geriatric	symmetrical	osteopath
striation	pendulous	kaiser
Appaloosa	analepsis	imperious
ramifications	mitigative	Egyptian
temerity	pyrite	foible
egress	sacrifice	lousicide
geocaching	consternation	ewer
instigate	escalator	curfew
obscure	impasto	schism
transcription	antagonistic	dilapidated

**preferred spelling

Who Knew?

The Scripps National Spelling Bee is the nation's largest and longest-running educational program.

peony
urgency
bifurcate
drivel
jettison
Promethean
embassy
contemptuous
okapi
welterweight

scrooge
morose
osmosis
flimflammer
astringent
mademoiselle
nouveau
heterochromia
consul
hermetically

excursion
dreadlocks
theriatrics
cumbersome
affluent
chastise
colic
atomic
fêng shui
acuity

subliminal
charismatic
phoenix
bastion
edamame
porcelain
deglaciation
recruit
tableau
sheldrake

suitable
cenotaph
Plumeria
perpetrator
cinematic
wallaby
contrivance
suffrage
thyme
phlebotomy

anemic
OR anaemic
depravity
effervescent
soirée
OR soiree
churros
diadem
larceny
acetaminophen

parochial
earnestly
**gaffe
OR gaff
ostensibly
gesticulate
gingivitis
patience
quittance
tenement

soothsayer
varicose
adage
cicada
mauve
emeritus
suture
obfuscate
casualty
perseverance

apparatus
myopic
ebullience
clairvoyance
impetus
affianced
archaism
commodious
austere
severance

**preferred spelling

financier	inimical	alma mater
wildebeest	kaleidoscope	comedienne
asado	gluttonous	cutaneous
limpa	gypsum	gnarled
adolescence	polypeptide	hydroponic
menagerie	wushu	combustible
hallucinate	contradictory	factorial
opprobrious	penitentiary	dolma
nocturnal	umbrage	sapphire
redolent	crustaceans	prevenient
vendage	bubonic	Edenic
entente	sartorial	tributary
boomslang	escarpment	laudatory
circuitous	Celsius	jitney
veracity	dialysis	wattage
marionette	humidistat	papillon
Neapolitan	sardonic	vertigo
chintzy	braille	accumulate
genteel	vignette	deltoidal
requisition	adjudicate	opulent
stimuli	caricature	paramecium
schooner	emerald	monochrome
declamatory	liege	facade
embryo	wilco	OR façade
languorous	germane	evaporation
stevia	bacteriolytic	bittern
phycology	rhododendron	flotsam
malaise	ineptitude	discombobulate
staid	academese	scrutiny
acerbity	registrar	concatenate

Did You Know?

In 2002, the Bee introduced the written test at the national finals for the first time. The vocabulary portion of the test came along in 2013.

---

impeachable	proletarian	adieu
residue	vantage	tenaciously
halibut	discountenance	indemnity
spectrometer	stupefy	cyanosis
circadian	irrevocable	regurgitate
servitude	trellis	stegosaur
traverse	juxtapose	statuesque
tungsten	hydrangea	nectarine
vineyard	slalom	galvanize
interrogative	corollary	agonistic
scullery	étude	rosin
tiramisu	cranium	burial
exaggerate	equivalent	bulwark
enoki	portentous	iridescent
profundity	nepotism	quince
mantra	truffle	cyclone
escarole	varicella	usurper
nanotechnology	tonsillitis	phraseology
bureau	thoracic	caramel
burglarious	proviso	pecuniary
cryptozoa	netiquette	cornea
preponderance	paucity	resilience
bruxism	doldrums	apiary
psychoanalysis	slumgullion	ronin
calendar	valedictorian	tropical
reiterate	auspices	pontiff
remorseful	elaborative	omniscient
cybernetics	proprietary	capacity
garniture	**nascent	sewage
twilight	OR naissant	epoxy

**preferred spelling

discreetly
sieve
trounce
hydrophobia
ingot
nubuck
jocularity
unfurl
calculator
corduroy

encore
hollyhock
qualms
mosaic
centipede
attendee
nomenclature
botany
Holocaust
augment

acoustic
eruption
auburn
virtually
glissando
stomach
demonstrative
megalomaniac
posse
declension

berserk
cathedral
deciduous
baleen
Einstein
municipal
adversaria
turbinado
brethren
tympanum

fisticuffs
propinquity
epidermis
carriage
abstemious
echinoderm
optimum
pathogen
acrostic
anthropology

cruciferous
macchiato
ancillary
toile
plaudits
serenade
heptad
engineer
pilcrow
porosity

tandoori
succumb
fervently
divestiture
roseola
installation
harbinger
raptatorial
sobriety
manumit

dentifrice
collegiality
inclement
celery
idiosyncratic
burgoo
occupancy
coriander
amnesty
condensation

aqueduct
ferret
widdershins
hostile
subsequent
whet
blatant
pyramid
terminus
agitation

tremulous
scythe
duplicitous
protectorate
placards
corral
credulity
dissonance
shoji
auditorium

reconcilable
evaluate
mastodon
denticulate
supplicate
torsion
justiciable
vernal
aardvark
census

stagflation
brontophobia
macrobiotics
glareous
rejuvenate
tubular
dodecahedron
rictus
vengeance
modular

kleptocrat
neuropathy
surrealist
secession
digression
intricate
annotate
vehemence
fervorous
septennial

hypotenuse
emancipatory
supine
fracas
disrepair
photogenic
rehearsal
irritability
vainglorious
ataxia

pageantry
vinegar
fiduciary
emulsify
lorikeet
malfeasance
sequential
intersperse
numerology
Paleozoic

funnel
syndicate
chrysalis
bethesda
cartilage
coeval
curio
ombudsman
hydrant
zeppelin

superficiality
marooned
**volary
OR volery
follicle
brochure
grotesqueness
privatim
eradicate
krypton

ethanol
quadriceps
tachycardia
triceratops
sandal
pashmina
utilitarian
millivolt
herringbone
orchestra

**preferred spelling

phlox	boondoggle	wordmonger
tractability	phylum	wobbulator
montage	hypochondria	mahogany
compendium	obstetrician	moribund
unmoored	replete	recriminatory
yardang	raucous	subaqueous
fluctuation	Brandywine	recusancy
flabbergast	surreptitious	retrocedence
accolade	surplus	cauterize
connivery	impediment	immolate
impresario	revenant	résumé
bruschetta	topgallant	extensive
dictum	clandestine	transcend
premonition	genealogical	freneticism
stereotypical	pomposity	merino
bergamot	neonatology	pestilence
telepathic	pituitary	mordant
banquet	fleetness	posthumous
upbraid	anonymity	QWERTY
pancreas	carcinogenic	foosball
expunge	detritus	accentuate
maize	anorak	ascension
metastasize	enviable	venue
quintessential	extrapolate	microfiche
pollutant	extinguish	quadrilateral
brouhaha	pilaster	turpentine
pedantry	perceptible	cellophane
performance	dystopia	indulgent
equivocate	muesli	occipital
fission	crux	predicament

From Around the World

Most spellers at the Scripps National Spelling Bee are from the United States, but spellers also come from American Samoa, Guam, Puerto Rico, the U.S. Virgin Islands, Department of Defense Schools in Europe as well as the Bahamas, Canada, Ghana, Jamaica, Japan and South Korea.

provincial	clowder	casserole
antithesis	occultation	semester
gouge	Chihuahua	sacrament
salivate	promontory	terra-cotta
laity	shar-pei	moratorium
indolent	narcoleptic	cognizant
documentary	efface	OR *cognisant
bromide	sycophant	languish
algae	bellwether	protuberant
reminiscent	clarinet	chortle
menial	capillary	unscathed
Moroccan	disposition	raclette
clearance	remonstrance	superstitious
assure	smithereens	mawkish
compatriots	curator	flambé
liaise	judicious	patronymic
quotidian	vice versa	odometer
matriculation	exercise	uvula
revulsive	civet	enumerated
gaucho	pancetta	desertification
capsule	waiver	quirky
tragedian	decennial	arraign
fajitas	dynamite	elegant
felonious	Gemini	minacious
palatial	retinol	vindictive
Mecca	corpulent	implacable
albeit	potpourri	logarithmic
vermicide	pallor	regicide
echelon	Yorkshire	hubris
supremacy	Belgravia	hibernaculum

*chiefly British spelling

The First Bee

In 1925, the first national spelling bee was organized by the *Louisville Courier-Journal* with a total of nine spellers. Frank Neuhauser won the championship title after correctly spelling "gladiolus."

bandicoot
malinger
parliamentary
rebarbative
olympiad
crocodile
venerable
chemise
campanology
persuasible

desultorily
papyrus
El Niño
anchorage
conundrum
debilitate
mittimus
mellifluous
clemency
backgammon

intuitable
divvy
fatuously
fraudulent
necessity
piety
veritable
sashay
sciatica
discomfiture

emphysema
stridency
acetone
cerebellum
pantomime
prima donna
praxis
Tinseltown
sorrel
McCoy

histrionics
cashier
polysemy
stampede
forfeit
armadillo
overweening
sacrosanct
syringe
eclipse

espadrille
corgi
caffeine
panacea
cabaret
froufrou
eschew
ventricle
inducement
vanguard

portrait
tepidity
meridian
spontaneity
platinum
nonnegotiable
disparate
artifice
cymbals
nucleated

exorbitant
reparations
constabulary
speculate
stratosphere
noxious
arbitrary
quasar
Podunk
seize

pathos
equinox
prosperous
sclerosis
ablaut
anabolic
jimberjawed
toilsome
tempestuous
univocal

avarice
bouclé
OR boucle
thoroughbred
potassium
peculate
treatise
undergird
oompah
adulation

minutia
anticipatory
chinook
indigent
merganser
sternum
par excellence
thwartwise
tae kwon do
fenestrated

lugubrious
isosceles
hoity-toity
Mesopotamian
Muzak
vicinity
merely
abominable
procedure
limpid

syllabus
animus
trillium
Dalmatian
ufology
cholera
**minuscule
OR miniscule
jeepney
volucrine

populace
vetiver
parameters
inflammable
pyrotechnics
mollify
cohesive
stigmata
prolix
mitochondria

onomatopoeia
lavender
tensile
gaudery
luxuriate
cavalcade
gladiatorial
machination
pugnacious
peruse

alluvial
epicurean
derelict
revelation
arithmetic
depredation
ignominious
auction
assiduous
diligence

bodega
bona fide
gustatory
obliterate
legalese
rudiments
monitory
equilibrium
roustabout
trifle

ambrosial
simultaneity
gastronome
epithet
encroach
acacia
tetanus
scarlatina
ciao
genome

**preferred spelling

Did You Know?
The Scripps National Spelling Bee was featured in the Academy Award-nominated documentary *Spellbound*.

inviolable
contrite
patrician
enervate
turophile
Patagonia
vanquish
ectoplasm
olfactory
en masse

stroganoff
procrastinate
purification
plantain
aperture
rhythmically
dovecote
bountiful
pantheon
marimba

conduit
bravado
beneficent
indict
epitome
annulment
vegetarian
surimi
besmirch
trespass

commandeer
bonsai
university
celestial
preposterous
extant
cogently
auricular
settee
legitimately

inoculate
heleoplankton
pliant
billiards
obstreperous
frabjous
spiracle
Formica
Mylar
rustication

globular
stellular
akimbo
derisive
ineluctable
eerily
funambulist
apotheosis
entrée
homeostasis

calamari
prehensile
somatotype
bizarro
dissemble
gallant
intensify
hurriedly
corrosive
afghan

odontiasis
stratification
tomahawk
artesian
mendacious
gubernatorial
pungent
mandrill
gibbous
extracurricular

punctuation
nautilus
thievery
dragoon
yuzu
ritziness
gazette
continuum
pachyderm
symposium

floribunda
salience
molasses
classical
fungible
Gothamite
affable
dopamine
pitiful
ammunition

pariah
prodigious
denominator
prorogue
fecund
laceration
nexus
decor
OR décor
duchy

pagoda
establishment
ruminate
sympathy
puniness
lingua franca
triforium
**déjà vu
OR déjà vue
calabash

**chute
OR shute
impermeable
trepidation
collision
scarab
veganism
humerus
vagabonds
variegated

volition
gossamer
vincible
factitious
sculpture
annuity
quid pro quo
curmudgeon
cushion
tutelage

domiciled
theorem
accrual
grandeur
ottoman
logographic
armistice
cryogenic
catalyst
thespian

submersible
extemporaneous
ungetatable
unilaterally
ordinance
ursine
arduous
carnitas
bulgogi
fibromyalgia

terrier
captivated
onus
precursor
mochi
feign
dementia
voilà
OR voila
habanero

Francophone
convivium
atrium
italicization
preliminary
echoed
reticulated
authenticate
fiscal
oblige

**preferred spelling

viscount
plague
preferential
bazooka
complacency
kraken
stanzaic
putrescent
nostalgia
dechlorinate

unconscionable
Pembroke
liquefaction
palazzo
miasma
concoct
modicum
javelin
spoonerism
complicit

gyrocopter
**medieval
OR mediaeval
licensure
Herculean
pilgrimages
oriel
preeminent
alfresco
loquacious

prosthetic
latency
epitaphs
solitaire
dishevel
Limburger
tuffet
epact
abstruse
nephrolith

adipose
quorum
pharynx
epistolary
pursuit
esoteric
grapheme
trigonometry
alloy
Belgium

audacious
exasperate
Mandarin
Kelvin
vellum
enunciate
tarsier
autodidact
parable
rowan

tripartite
Bohemian
succinct
inquietude
compunction
decumbiture
multivalent
artillery
quotient
ricotta

guttural
atrocious
vivacious
xenoglossy
smorgasbord
electrode
sporadically
sudation
cytoplasm
affectionately

Pulitzer
vitreous
wraith
insulin
phlegmatic
spasmodic
bouquet
denizen
duopoly
alpinist

**preferred spelling

abracadabra	abhenry	jonquil
plethora	chromosome	pensive
rappelled	braggart	quarantine
conceit	relentlessly	schnitzel
tapas	opalescence	rialto
sediment	polyglot	delphinium
emulate	velociraptor	obelisk
caveat	puree	diurnal
doubloons	manticore	prejudice
oscillation	chronometer	bombastic
enzyme	cherubic	cistern
dinero	wherewithal	exquisite
comestibles	inquisitor	epsilon
stenographer	chemistry	petroglyphs
mezzanine	quandary	specious
lozenge	equanimity	pumice
tedious	thermos	zodiac
resonate	acrylics	artery
suspicion	imminent	ornithology
repudiate	hieroglyphics	apropos
emporium	oculus	pessimum
Victorian	dubiously	amateurish
forestallment	mariposa	**intransigent
Iberian	teleology	OR intransigeant
fluency	bowyer	tyrannical
invective	infatuation	pearlescent
occur	abysmal	tautology
claustrophobia	chambray	misconstrue
idyllic	rhombus	sagacious
coralline	revendicate	mammalian

**preferred spelling

There's a First Time for Everything
Hugh Tosteson was the first winner from outside of the fifty U.S. states. He lived in Puerto Rico.

---

tranquil
behemoth
equestrian
nominal
draconian
trebuchet
ransom
iambic
monocle
apocalypse

cemetery
anticoagulant
euro
Gouda
endocrine
presumptuous
doubt
unkempt
cursive
binoculars

apportion
gurney
sanctimonious
peremptory
infarction
cedar
udon
gourd
verbatim
joule

niacin
courage
arabesque
cylindrical
tephra
lackadaisical
silhouette
dismal
consortium
tuition

multifarious
unanimous
soporific
tupelo
cadaverous
prowess
dromedary
squalid
tracheotomy
firmament

paramountcy
sultana
agrarian
collapsar
exhibition
ministrations
racketeer
solder
interim
definiendum

rhubarb
neutron
epigram
marmoset
panache
lucrative
bardolatry
scrimshaw
pterodactyl
inculcate

nimbostratus
vertebral
racial
acrimony
certitude
mimeograph
territory
ultimatum
ambidexterity
mortgage

exhaust
baroque
gonzo
strengthen
ostracism
hasten
bossa nova
rationale
betrothal
laminate

laborious	gosling	urbanely
sententious	optometry	lanai
cardiopathy	niche	hyacinth
vanity	paragon	segmentate
nymphal	foliage	convalesce
grammarian	tribunal	vagary
empirical	apostate	devoid
havoc	plundered	promulgate
figurative	multitude	salinity
malacology	enthalpy	analogize
saskatoon	truculence	guineas
enmity	quagmire	conglomerate
undulating	masseuse	**baklava
circumscribe	Hippocratic	OR baklawa
ensemble	warrior	ipso facto
bassoon	brachiopods	coupon
preamble	macaroon	signatory
feasibility	brazenness	aspirate
jurisdiction	beautician	senator
mycology	covetous	angular
antelope	flippancy	concomitant
mansard	sequester	sundry
Stilton	sufficiency	salutary
barracks	wayward	indubitable
rendition	yeoman	obituary
calories	Websterian	obsidian
sortition	grievance	bidialectal
ballistic	solemn	officiant
nattily	zealous	annexation
tincture	portcullis	animalier

**preferred spelling

endogenous
Beefalo
pavlova
malleable
idiolect
irascible

Eight Times the Fun

In 2019, eight spellers made Bee history and inspired a neologism: "Octochamps!" At about midnight on the night of the Finals, the dictionary admitted defeat to what the Bee declared "the most phenomenal assemblage of spellers in the history of this storied competition." Rishik Gandhasri, Erin Howard, Saketh Sundar, Shruthika Padhy, Sohum Sukhatankar, Abhijay Kodali, Christopher Serrao and Rohan Raja ended the 2019 Bee in an eight-way tie.

Difficulty Level: Three Bee
School Spelling Bee Study List

lacrosse	aspersions	Apollo
McIntosh	culminate	accordance
ignoble	helium	atmospheric
diaphoresis	steeplechasing	levees
kurta	Teflon	precariously
Hyperion	bantam	proportionate
Geiger	apprentice	suffused
thermohaline	reluctant	accelerates
gannet	heritage	coincidence
palladium	sojourner	prestigious
brevet	derogatory	emphatic
pamphlet	palsy	contaminated
palindrome	Lascaux	Madagascar
visite	synesthesia	exposure
satsuma	OR synaesthesia	parachuted
stirrups	nefarious	periodically
Connemara	halogens	intriguing
abundance	gallium	absorptive
calamitous	smelters	incomprehensible
dropsonde	hymnal	Merrimack
proclamation	tartaric	Sinai
hokum	bindi	asparagus
colossal	Haitian	solace
coltan	divan	argyria
squadron	badminton	guanine
marinate	bayonet	xylyl
anagrams	currycomb	therapeutic
verandas	haughty	tumultuous
OR verandahs	hesitate	commodore
Himalayan	opportunity	playwright

senile	Giza	denouncement
laryngitis	fixity	Columbia
proximo	jodhpurs	misdemeanor
**guerrilla	hydrargyrum	OR
OR guerilla	carborane	*misdemeanour

*chiefly British spelling
**preferred spelling

Bee's Bookshelf
The Bee's Bookshelf is the official online book club of the Scripps National Spelling Bee. It's a place to explore the connection between stories and spelling. Each month, we read a new book together and share insights, so sign up to receive our monthly emails to find out which book is next. Visit spellingbee.com/bookshelf to learn more.

Difficulty Level: Three Bee
Words of the Champions

imaret	sumpsimus	umami
cornichon	morel	persiflage
devastavit	abeyance	toreador
Mediterranean	rongeur	vermicelli
longevous	mountebank	frangipane
digerati	allelopathy	reseau
solecism	capoeira	moulage
hypertrophy	agnolotti	interpellate
ravigote	ballabile	genuflect
inchoate	draegerman	cinerarium
judoka	prescient	polemic
vaccary	Fribourg	paladin
Adelaide	proselytizer	totipotency
unwonted	OR *proselytiser	agnomen
tazza	tenon	Bauhaus
damson	nubilous	sacerdotal
pelisse	iatrogenic	skeuomorph
succade	onychitis	binturong
tumulus	roux	mamushi
dorsiflexor	tuatara	lipophilic
profiterole	chicle	codicil
valetudinary	sulcus	coulomb
aristoi	thalamus	violaceous
vireo	gyttja	Rorschach
rococo	jibboom	arthralgia
lachsschinken	vestigial	desman
wakame	Orwellian	jacaranda
bathos	gimbaled	huapango
nihilism	cabaletta	predilection
ustion	hesped	entomophagy

*chiefly British spelling

paronomasia	immure	maxillae
facsimile	theodicy	pseudonymous
renminbi	politeia	gentian
interferon	canard	synod
sedulous	Lisztian	pompadour
velouté	gerundial	quatrefoil
Aesopian	ensilage	pasquinade
frigate	cabal	Valkyrian
enoptromancy	sotto voce	zymurgy
satiety	inesculent	histolysis
perorate	cicerone	penurious
**imbroglio	pusillanimous	Magellan
OR embroglio	quidnunc	Reykjavík
ochlocracy	genoise	moussaka
brioche	arachnophagous	serricorn
adumbrate	pirouetted	Nereid
depilatory	bestial	oyez
bucolic	hallux	Huguenot
milieu	jabot	acequia
woad	saponaceous	adrenergic
terpsichore	cyrillic	habitué
strychnine	Adélie	OR habitue
pissaladière	manteau	kalanchoe
nilpotent	framboise	warison
latitudinarian	littoral	carapace
voltammetry	jacana	dauerlauf
rathskeller	sommelier	emanant
asphyxiate	pikas	carte blanche
spondylitis	examen	bodhran
sequoia	plumassier	seiche

**preferred spelling

carmagnole
encina
encephalitis
ritenuto
effrontery
pastiche
almoner
caldera
querulous
hircine

rheumatic
risibility
Daliesque
prognosticate
gorgon
polydactyly
bireme
aposematic
bijouterie
inveighed

mostaccioli
azedarach
elision
danseur
chevalier
taurine
hierurgical
melee
emolument
ikebana

exaugural
gaillardia
caryatid
heliacal
schefflera
contrapposto
temblor
insouciance
catarrh
quattrocento

millegrain
canaille
verisimilitude
Keynesian
akaryote
azulejo
hauberk
bouillon
tarpaulin
cephalopod

pulchritude
pekoe
patois
Rubicon
bourgeois
aerophilatelic
ankh
contumelious
vicissitudes
lilliputian

Sbrinz
kathakali
cozen
oxalis
myeloma
lebensraum
mufti
dirigible
surcease
ascetic

oolite
revanche
megrims
podagra
palaver
luthier
yttriferous
vermeil
Ouagadougou
bibliopegist

plagiarism
holobenthic
boutonniere
anodyne
saccharide
boulevardier
quokka
lidocaine
contretemps
a posteriori

One Dictionary to Rule them All
The only source for the Scripps National Spelling Bee is the Merriam-Webster Unabridged Online Dictionary. (http://unabridged.merriam-webster.com/)

scaberulous
anaglyphy
reconnoiter
OR reconnoitre
realpolitik
colloque
onychorrhexis
paraffin
vigneron
tannined

spiedini
anhinga
jai alai
Rastafarian
succussion
avifauna
joropo
toxicosis
colporteur
OR colporter

agitprop
Achernar
cassock
meringue
mackinaw
sambal
yuloh
hermeneutics
tikkun
macaque

lassitude
oeuvre
altazimuth
Castilian
trichinosis
ecclesiology
teppanyaki
cicatrize
somnolent
intonaco

realia
grison
phulkari
garrulous
paroxysm
communiqué
Chantilly
jacquard
sorghum
guilloche

appositive
dirndl
latke
martinet
asterion
hypallage
solenoid
veridical
threnody
Jacobean

ballotage
ocotillo
dubitante
disciform
mizuna
trichotillomania
huipil
mustelid
prestidigitation
soupçon

diphtheria
bdelloid
nugatory
commorients
immiscible
toroidal
bialy
appurtenances
corsair
zabaglione

velamen
sporran
clematis
kente
ranine
riparian
**accoutrement
OR accouterment
radicchio

**preferred spelling

dudgeon
nitid
Basenji
concinnate
Stradivarius
synecdoche
tulsi
sebaceous
papeterie
litigious

phytophilous
meunière
hilum
fanfaronade
malachite
urticaria
capsaicin
ptosis
pejerrey
horologist

speleothem
euripus
samarium
variscite
bolide
vervain
chanoyu
hamadryad
calumny
escabeche

ad hominem
oubliette
béchamel
repoussage
otacoustic
naranjilla
elegiac
pâtissier
OR patissier
Yeatsian

surfeit
limicolous
girandole
googol
étagère
anechoic
leonine
laulau
Gruyère
proprioceptive

oppugn
macropterous
euphonious
retinoscopy
sepulchral
sangfroid
pasilla
maringouin
argot
vicenary

ajimez
pompeii
oviparous
mangonel
coalescence
Plantagenet
bauxite
kakapo
pelagial
ague

largesses
fulgent
olecranon
toreutics
mascarpone
rissole
seneschal
pinniped
wahine
grissino

coterie
sylph
katsura
diastole
mediobrome
demurrage
tristeza
trigeminal
bruja
upsilon

It's All Greek to Me

We often get questions about why we use words that may not appear to be English. Most words in the English language are words that we borrowed from other languages. We borrowed them, used them, and now call them our own.

sakura
buccal
zocalo
**aficionado
OR afficionado
piscivorous
benison
gagaku
amygdala
scurrilous

flèche
tetrachoric
sforzando
thalassic
frazil
rapprochement
glacis
ahimsa
kanji
weltschmerz

jalousie
ichthyology
pruritus
dactylic
affogato
scrivener
dysrhythmia
dragée
choucroute
hsaing-waing

stevedore
harangue
niveau
rouille
rescissible
Jungian
Groenendael
facile
chrysolite
execrable

hangul
cartouches
Nicoise
OR Niçoise
julienne
moiety
pastitsio
modiste
deuterium
Icarian

pappardelle
Sahel
bibelot
telegnosis
loupe
oleiculture
**loess
OR löss
ruelle
Ushuaia

redingote
adscititious
hummock
internecine
duxelles
mesial
Feldenkrais
bailiwick
bozzetto
coiffure

repartee
chimera
OR *chimaera
avgolemono
exiguous
presentient
renvoi
kichel
semaphore
gambol

angiitis
Teutonic
Conestoga
zeitgeist
heinousness
nacelle
rupicolous
Pythagorean
kepi
**bulgur
OR bulghur

*chiefly British spelling
**preferred spelling

ushabti	hirsute	cygnet
puchero	shubunkin	supercilious
nival	hepatectomy	dysphasia
ascites	bloviate	kugel
Véronique	seine	topazolite
OR Veronique	galapago	trompe l'oeil
planetesimal	au courant	ailette
taoiseach	crepuscular	fetticus
obeisant	theca	rocaille
whippoorwill	croustade	couverture
Ficus	kipuka	lemniscus
agelicism	noumenon	ad nauseam
subrident	chicanery	ganache
ethylene	vilipend	sauger
flaneur	vitiate	kanban
Ponzi	spodumene	toccata
teneramente	leberwurst	pertinacity
styptic	daguerreotype	gasthaus
sopapilla	yakitori	transmontane
nictitate	pejorate	laterigrade
boutade	Aitutakian	hyssop
towhee	parterre	naumachia
escritoire	rondeau	focaccia
affenpinscher	atlatl	pahoehoe
gudgeon	allochroous	Kjeldahl
beaumontage	ennui	rubefacient
galoot	caisson	halcyon
desiccate	cheongsam	corrigenda
aporia	graticule	Zanni
moraine	gyascutus	nonage

beurre	tiffin	unguiculate
jicama	colcannon	amaryllis
sturnine	tournedos	reveille
octonocular	ormolu	regnal
parallax	blottesque	attaché
antenatus	consommé	rafflesia
trouvaille	OR consomme	ranunculus
glazier	ullage	pistou
kinesiology	zortzico	scintillation
exogenous	teratism	Bolognese
aniseikonia	flagellum	farrago
guayabera	panegyric	coup de grace
realgar	hoi polloi	tourelle
anaphylaxis	sirenian	notturno
bobolink	nescience	ginglymus
diluent	blatherskite	hemorrhage
urushiol	consigliere	tapetum
andouille	adiabatic	golem
otiose	camembert	krewe
megacephalic	ecchymosis	toque
souchong	oppidan	avuncular
poltroon	decastich	habiliments
Freudian	Naugahyde	rubato
floruit	lefse	gentilitial
Bunyanesque	beccafico	obnebulate
exsect	amphistylar	allonym
champignon	saturnine	croquembouche
bahuvrihi	zaibatsu	kobold
panjandrum	titian	mendicity
catachresis	tokonoma	castellated

Home Sweet Home
While many people think the Bee is headquartered in Washington, D.C., our hive is actually located in Cincinnati, Ohio.

---

toponymic
boudin
bucatini
reboation
haupia
Keplerian
codswallop
hauteur
camarilla
nidicolous

oxyacetylene
queue
hellebore
transhumance
phloem
lacustrine
ageusia
pillor
deleterious
ikat

pylorus
erythroblast
maillot
epenthesis
hinoki
nonpareil
nyctinasty
pointelle
vinaigrette
tinnient

aioli
pochoir
glyceraldehyde
hagiographer
syncope
icosahedron
goanna
wassail
ammonite
tanager

pneumatocyst
fortissimo
portmanteau
coaxation
ardoise
farouche
farfalle
ogival
stretto
coccygeal

Diplodocus
tachyon
piccata
isagoge
élan
breviloquence
kalimba
illative
betony
bêtise

transience
frison
flavedo
maquillage
mortadella
stanchion
spirulina
eleemosynary
force majeure
ossicle

anemone
alpargata
disembogue
luculent
expatiate
xerogel
vizierial
crescive
tryptophan
neophyte

buffa
clavichord
de rigueur
secant
comanchero
meiosis
gules
nimiety
lokelani
psoriasis

bavardage	foudroyant	farina
coulibiac	sesquipedalian	heuristic
xyloglyphy	expugnable	nudibranch
Aramaic	profligacy	triquetra
anathema	yosenabe	paramahamsa
basilica	funori	duello
rajpramukh	piloncillo	fjeld
Chalcolithic	xiphias	tomography
rinceau	étouffée	effleurage
filar	OR etouffee	chastushka
bhangra	degauss	bergère
risorgimento	tussock	Erewhonian
agalma	lanolated	rhyton
analgesia	linnet	orogeny
dengue	embouchure	Pepysian
cantatrice	plangency	esplanade
emollient	apocryphal	gesellschaft
parquet	tamarack	tamari
dhurrie	puerilely	arenaceous
lapidary	obloquy	panettone
cachexia	dhole	tmesis
connoisseur	**budgerigar	clerihew
ferruginous	OR budgereegah	tsukupin
gendarme	OR budgerygah	katakana
demulcent	outré	Parmentier
goosander	ululate	rugose
kwashiorkor	sororal	brume
lecithin	epideictic	hiortdahlite
cetology	embolus	extravasate
plenipotentiary	caveola	incunabula

**preferred spelling

cordillera
zazen
cabochon
après
zydeco
consanguine
bibimbap
aquiclude
demitasse
tomalley

bouffant
bas-relief
rhizome
Wensleydale
erubescent
estovers
rembrandt
bonspiel
hackamore
blancmange

simulacrum
cnidarian
capotasto
Panagia
nockerl
rhabdoid
apodyterium
apoplexy
verdure
fait accompli

dreikanter
penicillin
pendeloque
beelzebub
rhinorrhagia
Foley
syzygy
Beethovenian
tatterdemalion
susurrus

**bienvenue
OR bienvenu
potwalloper
kaffeeklatsch
peregrination
paraquat
prana
sinciput
abattoir
glossopetrae

diktat
llanero
Machiavellian
glaucomatous
haori
rheostat
hariolation
thylacine
cenote
griffonage

fossiliferous
calefacient
obdurate
nunchaku
senryu
cormorant
gnomon
pinetum
brucellosis
wasteweir

diamanté
sphygmometer
**kibitzer
OR kibbitzer
auteur
labefaction
ibidem
estival
OR aestival
loup-garou

empennage
lysozyme
grimthorpe
thaumaturge
pinioned
fouetté
venenate
badinage
saccadic
mignonette

**preferred spelling

coadjutor	harmattan	tralatitious
chiffonade	**incarnadine	denouement
haricot	OR encarnadine	hortatory
Luddite	dulcinea	maquette
wickiup	nainsook	obliviscence
nisse	querida	autophagy
impugn	paillard	Airedale
brouillon	gazoz	potager
derecho	Glaswegian	malleolus
solipsist	stannum	
sinophile	putsch	

**preferred spelling

Word Club

Want a new way to study? The Word Club app, launching in October 2019 in the App Store and the Google Play Store, will make mastering Words of the Champions fun! Choose from multiple different quiz and study options for both spelling and vocabulary, all with expert audio pronunciations from the Bee's official pronouncer, Dr. Jacques Bailly.

About Scripps

The E.W. Scripps Company (NASDAQ: SSP) serves audiences and businesses through a growing portfolio of local and national media brands. With 52 television stations in 36 markets, Scripps is one of the nation's largest independent TV station owners. Scripps runs a collection of national journalism and content businesses, including Newsy, the next-generation national news network; podcast industry leader Stitcher; the fast-growing national broadcast networks Bounce, Grit, Escape, Laff and Court TV; and Triton, the global leader in digital audio technology and measurement services. Scripps runs an award-winning investigative reporting newsroom in Washington, D.C., and is the longtime steward of the Scripps National Spelling Bee. Founded in 1878, Scripps has held for decades to the motto, "Give light and the people will find their own way."

Made in the USA
Coppell, TX
17 November 2019